CW01665414

For The Love of You

Written by Victoria Sneade

Illustrated by Vicky Moran and Grace Abela

For The Love of You

Written by Victoria Sneade
Illustrated by Vicky Moran & Grace Abela

First published in 2023

ISBN: 978-1-3999-6877-5

TAUK
Publishing

DEDICATION

To the ones who have no voice.

For The Love of You

These poems were created with all in mind.
Within even one poem, I hope you will find
A message of love to pour into your soul
FOR IT'S THE LOVE OF YOU that should be your primary goal

When you find that your self-love is in overflow
And your self-care is somewhat complete
Then go share the overflow with everyone else
And pass the LOVE on to whomever you meet

Love Vicky

The Jade Roberts Project

For each book sold, I will donate a percentage of the sales to the Jade Roberts Project.

The number of deaths recorded shows that suicide is one of the highest causes of death, and the Jade Roberts Project work tirelessly to help people with their mental health. They specialise in suicide intervention and offer one-to-one counselling and support to anyone who has experienced a loss through suicide. The work they do is truly exceptional.

If you or anyone you know is experiencing difficulty with their mental health or has suicidal thoughts. Contact: info@thejaderobertsproject.co.uk or on 0151 245 5671.

Don't forget what truly matters is you.

www.gofund.me/865b359d

Contents

If Only

Life isn't always what we expect it to be
I can hear my head constantly talking to me.
If only you'd lived in a different way
Your life would be so much better today.

If only I'd focused more at school
And not always been just playing the fool.
If only I'd not portrayed the spoilt child
Or in my teenage years, so rampant and wild.

If only I'd kept the drugs and alcohol at bay
My life could have been so different today.
If only my family were more spiritually connected
I believe that my ways would have been spiritually corrected.

I could have been a director of a company I owned
I could have been healthy and evenly toned.
I often think of how I'd like to have been wed
And to have travelled the world from A to Z.

All my if only's can be my deepest regrets
But it's time to turn my *could haves* into maybe *not yets.*
SO
Regret turns into excitement as I wonder what will be
Just what's around the corner, I'm excited to see.

Ruminating my *if onlys* won't ever change the past
With my connection to my spirit, I now see this at last.
This life I get once; therefore, I must move on
The present is here and my past is gone.

'Let go of the regrets and choose the what yets'

A Name With No Shame

A name is just a name
Yet I feel shame in my name.
Would I prefer my name if I were a Dame?
One day, my name may come with some fame.
But that doesn't matter; it's not the fame that I need
Or seeing my name in the headlines of the papers we read.
You see, my name is connected to who I'm to be.
Caring yet wild, and so feisty and free.
SO
To put honour to my name is what I really desire
And to give you my innermost self.
So, I'd rather be remembered for my weird, wonderful ways
Than to be stuck in a frame on the shelf.
Doesn't matter what name I've been given
As long as I'm happy to be.
Victoria Sneade—yes, that's my name,
Now it's time to live on and be
ME.

'Be proud of who you are.'

To Beat or Not To Beat

I feel the pressure in the air
As his body sends off the heat.
He knows he's given the choice
To beat or not to beat.
First, the smack
Then a knock to the floor.
I ask in prayer
For help at my door.
A kick to the ribs
And then to the head.
It's times like this
I wish I were dead.
I feel no more blows
But I must stay still.
I know he's still angry
With an urge to kill.
I hear his footsteps
Moving away.
Thank you, God,
I hear myself say.

As I nurse my bruises
I start to cry.
As I look all around me
I ask myself why.
Why does he beat me?
And why do I stay?
Is it the hope
That he'll change someday?
I know I need money
And somewhere to stay.
I still pray for that courage
To just get away.
A few hours go by
The key turns in the door.
The fear runs through me
As I beg for no more.
'I'm so sorry, baby'
Are the words I hear.
He hands me the flowers
And says, 'There we go, dear.'
Time passes by
And the bruises are healed.
His lips touch mine
Now my memory is sealed.

SO

All seems to be well
And life seems good.
No longer does it feel
Like he's vying for my blood.
But weeks go by; it's that time again.
Don't think I can take anymore.
As I watch his temper rising
I make a run for the door.
I feel that pressure in the air
As his body sends off his heat.
But we all know he's given the choice
TO BEAT OR NOT TO BEAT.

'Remember! Everybody has a choice.'

Him

My stomach is churning when I think of him.
Is this a good thing or a bad thing?
It can't be good, as it makes me feel weak and dim.
Over and over and over again
I just seem to go with the same type of men.
What is it in me that feels compelled to experience the same?
Don't matter who *him* is.
They just own a different name.
You're too skinny.
You're too fat.
And you're too full of life.
Why don't you just marry me
And be grateful to be my wife?
These are the words I constantly hear.
My system just takes it like music to the ear.
Why do my thoughts not let me forget *him*?
Why do I always feel the need to return?
To a power that weakens me
And drains my vivaciousness.
Oh, why do I long to be with a *him*?

Oh, please, God, grant me the serenity to accept the things
I cannot change
As I cannot change the *hims* of this world.
Nor can I change how they treat their girl.
The courage to change the things I can.
I'm going to find me a beautiful man.
I'm going to change my system in life
And then, who knows,
I may even be grateful to be his wife.
I'll find a man who will love me, care for me
And accept me for me.
SO
Just hang on one minute.
This cannot happen until I truly do see.
It's not about finding *him*
It's about finding *me.*
So, let's rewind and look at that again.
The courage to change the things I can
I'm going to find out who I *truly am.*
I'm going to change my system in me
And become who I was always meant to be.
I'm excited to see what I have in store
And look forward to getting to know myself more.

New adventures and ideas will be full to the brim
Now that I'm searching for *me*
And not searching for *him.*

'There are many types of men out there.

There's only one you.

Enjoy searching within.'

He'd Have to Be...

He'd have to be single
No woman in tow.
Hospital's a place I don't want to go.
He'd have to be good-looking.
He'd have to be fit.
He'd have to be funny and
Not talk shit!
He'd have to not shout.
He'd have to be calm.
He'd not raise his fists.
He'd just be pure charm.
He'd have to like footy
Whilst listening to me.
He'd have to like shopping
And realise nothing's for free.
He'd have to be faithful
And he'd have to show me,
That it can stay in his pants
Just where it should be.
He'd have to not sit
And pick his nose for hours.

For instead of the snot
I'd much prefer flowers.
He'd have to have hair
But not too much.
He'd have to be gentle
Within his touch.
He'd have to like cleaning.
He'd have to be clever.
He'd have to be civil
And cannot be named Trevor.
He'd have to not take
The paper the loo.
And then come and inform me
'Bout the size of his poo.
He'd have to not think
It funny and smart
When wafting my way
His big, smelly fart.
He'd have to not be racist.
He'd have to be fair.
He'd have to show me
Just how much he can care.
He'd have to not gamble.

He'd have to not smoke.

He'd have to not take drugs.

Oh, my…what a bloke.

SO

I'm sure it's now quite clear

For everyone to see.

For me to meet the man of my dreams,

Well…

He'd have to be…like

ME!

'What can I say!'

Heart to Heart

Let's have a heart-to-heart
Let's not rip each other's hearts apart.
It's your heart that gives you breath
And it's also your heart that can lead you to death.
Why don't we just sit down and talk?
Or maybe even go for a walk?
Why are we prepared to hurt each other's hearts?
It wasn't like this from the very start.
SO
Now I've had enough
Of this trying to be tough.
This relationship's charred
And it makes my heart hard.
But my heart is *my* heart
I'm not letting it be torn apart.
I'm now going to start
Taking care of my heart.

'It's your heart that keeps you going.
Look after it.'

What I Want

Protection, not rejection, is what I want

And

Connection, not rejection, is what I want

And

Affection, not rejection, is what I want.

SO

Show me how you can protect me

And

Connect with me

And

How your love can positively affect me

That's what I want.

'You deserve all that's good.'

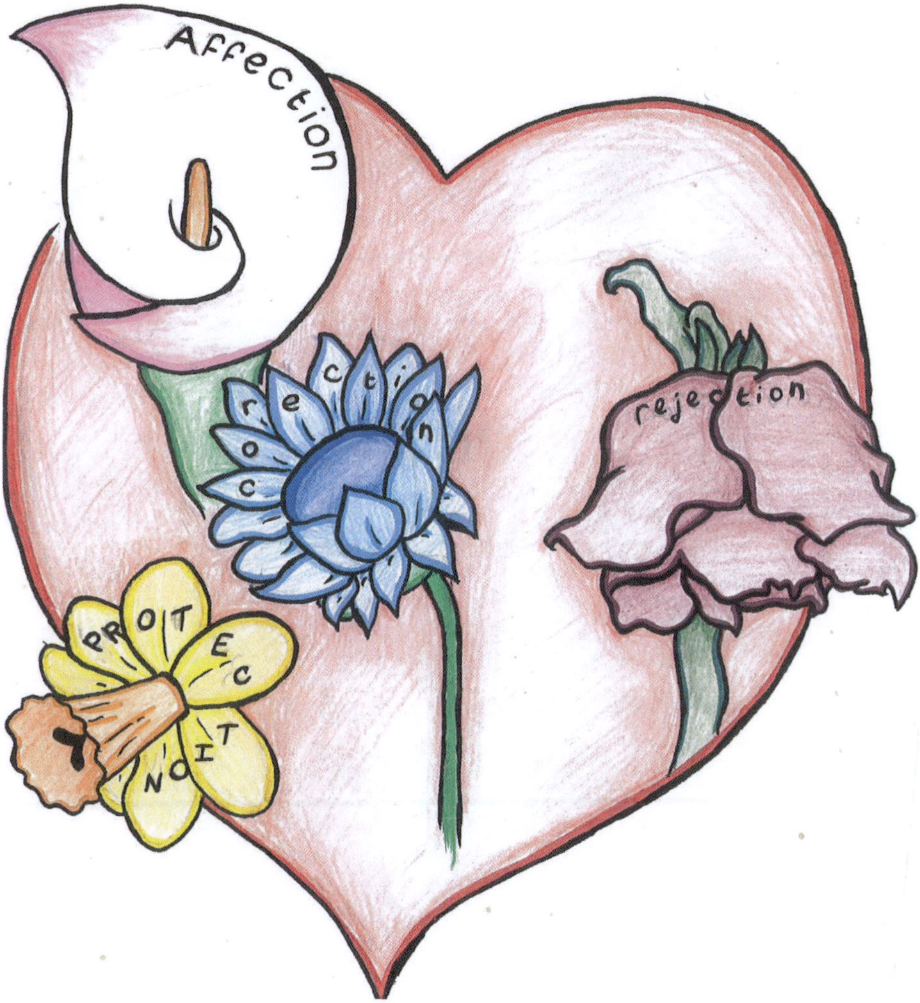

My Own Little Puppet

How foolish I was when I was a puppet
Being controlled by many of those strings.
You can call *your* strings whatever you want
But mine were all the wrong things.
How foolish I was when I was a puppet
Doing what I was told every day.
But not anymore; it's time for a *change*
And for me to do things my way.
SO
I'm now no longer their puppet
As I start to control my own strings.
With each conscious breath, I'm free to be me
And I'm choosing all the right things.
So *now* I'm my own little puppet
And I no longer desire their things.
You too can do this if you want to be free
Just let go and control your own strings.

'Let go and be free.'

Magnificent Me

That tree, that tree,
What a magnificent tree
Just standing so tall and as proud as can be.
I wish that was me
To be just like the tree.
Not worrying what people were thinking of me
And how cool would it be
To just go out and be ME.
Oh, my word NOOOO!
What would people think of that crazy me?
There you go again, not being able to be
People will see what they want to see.
SO
It's simple as and as plain as day
I was made in my own magnificent way.
It was always meant for me to be
Standing as proud as that magnificent tree.
AND
That I've been put on this earth.
To be MAGNIFICENT ME!

'Wow! Look at you!
How magnificent you look.'

Scouser Girl

I'm proud to be a Scouser
I'll never hide that from the world.
I'll shout it from the rooftops
That I'm a Scouser Girl.

So, what is it to be a Scouser
Let me tell you through my ode.
It starts with our Scouse humour
And comedians, we've had a load.

From Tarbuck through to Doddy
Paul'O Grady to Freddie Starr.
Stan Boardman, with his German jokes
And John Bishop beats Jimmy Carr.

But the latest to the Comedy Club
Paul Smith, yes, that's his name.
He's so genuinely funny
Ya see, humour is his game.

Then there's *that* John May
Now he's a funny man.
If ya haven't been to see him
Get to see him when ya can.

But we have naturally funny people
Across our city-wide.
We're so quick with our responses
Other cities, they have tried.

But they'll never be as quick
With their humour or their wit.
You see, you have to be a Scouser
And that's all there is to it.

We even rule the heart of music
From the Beatles to the La's.
And Frankie Goes to Hollywood
Now, these were proper stars.

Then there's Jamie Webster
Now there's a musical lad who knows.
Just how to get the point across
That with the Tories, nothing goes.

Then we have a DJ
Leanne Campbell is her name.
She brightens up our mornings
Without her, Radio City wouldn't be the same.

Then there's Leanne Campbell's teammate
We all know him as Scott Hughes.
He's our honorary Scouser
Of which, I'm sure, we all would choose.

Then we got ourselves Lee Butler
We all know Billy as his dad.
Lee's now got his own little station
In demand, ya are, lad.

We've got an MMA fighter
A Champion at his game.
We'll chant his name at football
'Cause he deserves the fame.

We know him as Paddy the Baddy
And ya don't wanna mess with him.
He'll have ya tapping on that floor
'Cause ya chance of winning is slim.

And then there's Meatball Molly
Another champion at keeping ya down.
If she ever wants to be my bodyguard
When I'm out and on the town.

We've even got our boxers
The Smiths, Fowler, and Bellew.
Their names are known so far and wide
But they're Scouse-bred through and through.

Now, football, there's a topic
Of one, we're proud to chat.
It doesn't matter which club you choose
We're Scousers, and that is that.

Liverpool or Everton
We're all just downright looney.
We had Carragher and Gerrard
Youse had Dixie Dean and Rooney.

And to all the other fans out there
Yes, we all do have a job.
Your chant is boring and very old
Get creative, or shut ya gob.

We get labelled that we're criers
But it's justice that we crave.
We have every right to get angry
When it's about lives we're fighting to save.

For those of you who want to say
That Scousers rob your tyres.
Oh, come on now, that's really weak
We'd rather have air fryers

We might have our wrong 'uns like anywhere else
But our good outweighs the bad.
And I'd rather be a Scouser
Ya see, I'm proud of me accent, lad.

Now, let's just add the other cities
In this little ode of mine.
You too can love your city
And that's absolutely fine.

But I'm so proud to be a Scouser
Just read the evidence above.
Makes it easy to see just why it is
Liverpool's the city I love.

'Be proud of where you're from.'

A Social Like Media

Hmm, it's time for a media post
What can I show?
It's usually all the things
I don't want you to know.
Insta is a place where I seem to compare
As I flick through their lives
I find I want to be her.
She's so much prettier
And she's got it all.
I so envy her life
And it makes me feel small.
I get hundreds of likes
But that doesn't matter.
It's the way that I feel
With that constant chatter.
That chatter that goes around in my head
It can take me to that place where I wish I were dead.
The anxiety gets stronger
And my heart starts to race.
Don't feel like I belong
And I can't find my place.

Does this sound familiar
To anyone out there?
Be it any social media
Anytime, anywhere.
SO
I really need to see this in a completely different way.
I really need to show you my true day-to-day.
I am who I am
That's how I was made.
If you don't like what you see
That's down to you, I'm afraid.
I can't ever change the way you see me.
So, no more comparing; I'm setting myself free.
Goodbye to the longing of me wanting to be you.
That's all a façade; not one bit of it true.
And hello to the woman that you're now going to see.
In fact, goodbye social media; it's time to be me.

'Don't compare. You're meant to be you.'

Sky Dancers

As I sit here in my sadness
Feels like my world is falling apart.
I look up and see the sky dancers
And something then touches my heart.

As I continue to watch the sky dancers
Begins to feel like my own private show.
As they dodge and they weave way up high
With no worries of where they may go.

The sky is their stage
And the sun is their light.
As they dance through the clouds
The sky dancers take flight.

As my music plays on
I see rhythm in their wings.
As if they are sent to remind me
Of one of the many wondrous things.

As the sun starts to go down

Their show still goes on.

I think I'll just sit here

'Til the sky dancers have gone.

'Remember to look up. You just never know what you may miss.'

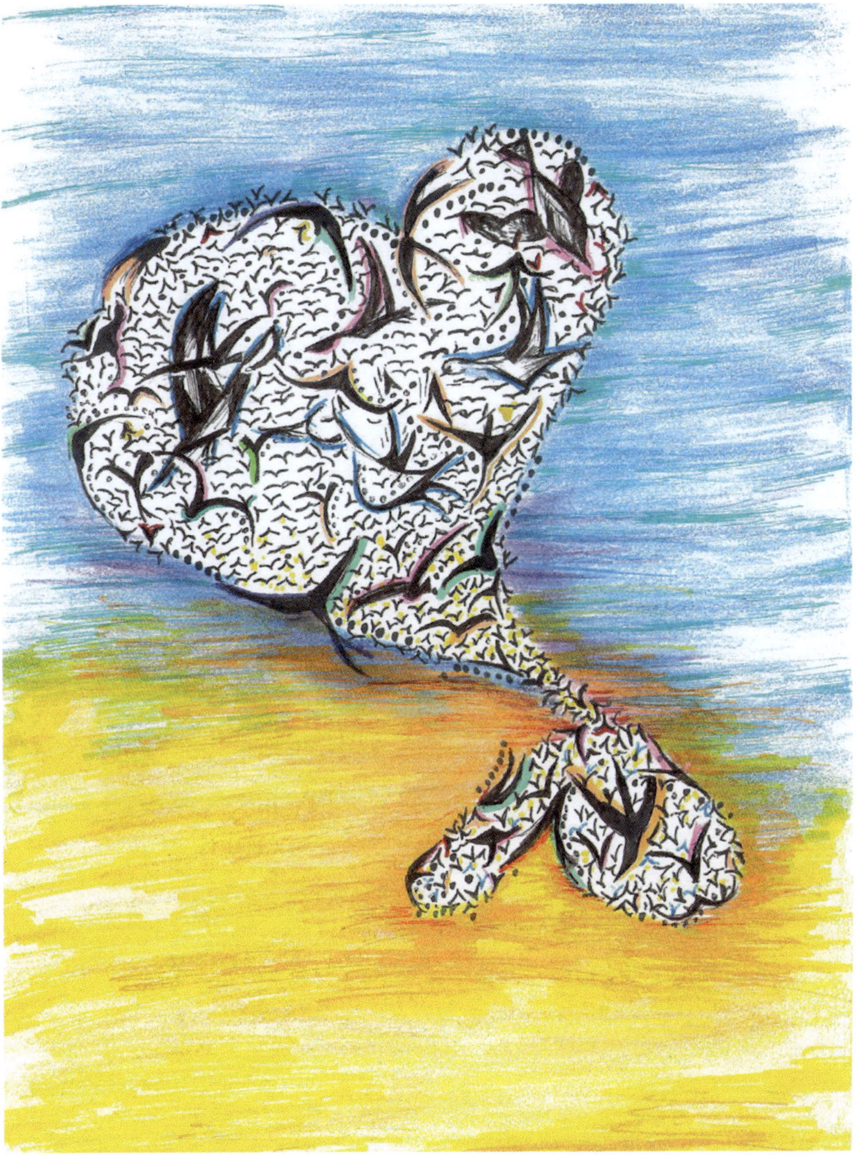

Your Hiding Sun

When it seems the sun is hiding
And your dreams seem hard to reach.
Remember that sun is shining
Over some distant golden beach.
When it seems the sun is hiding
Remember, it's somewhere there.
In those dark times you're experiencing
And it feels like no one cares.
When it seems the sun is hiding
And you no longer want to live.
Just take the time to remember
All that love you've got to give.
SO
When it seems the sun is hiding
And your hope for joy is gone.
Remember, it's within your heart
That the sun is shining on.
Cause someone else's sun is hiding
And they too feel in despair.

It's then that you reveal *your sun*
And show them that you care.

For it's when we share our shining sun
That our darkness turns to light.
No longer must our sun be hiding
For our future to be bright.

'Remember...your sun is there within you.
Keep shining.'

For The Love of You

SO

Whilst sitting and writing these poems
My desire within was to give
To anyone who reads them
A change in the way you may live.
From protecting your heart
To adoring your name.
For you to seek your own self
With no guilt and no shame.
To not only out the dark side
But to see the funny side too.
Of how you always strive for the best
When the best is always in you.
This you that needs to be nurtured
And loved so much to the core.
It's time to get rid of the negatives
That's what these poems are for.
May you say goodbye to the ego
And goodbye to those thoughts in your head.
That tell you you'd always be better off
Being somebody else instead.

You are magnificent just the way you are

Just like the magnificent tree

SO

Take off your veil and take a big breath

And go out into the world and BE

You!!

Love from

Victoria Sneade.

That's ME!

'There's only one you. Embrace every part.'

Acknowledgements

I would like to thank my children for being the beautiful souls they are and my grandson Luca for making my heart beat stronger.

I would like to thank my friends for always encouraging me to keep on.

Thank you to Grace and Vicky for taking the time to create such beautiful illustrations

Thank you to Jude Lennon for helping me to see we are all creative. It's just taking the time with oneself to truly see it.

A big thank you to Jo Abela, who gave me the kick to carry on with my dream. The memory of sitting at your dining table, ready to give up, but you would not let that happen. For that, I thank you.

Most of all, I would like to thank my resilience for helping me to bounce back from my adversities through life. It got me this far, and I ain't giving up now.

Love Vicky

Author Bio

Vicky was once, in her own words, caught up in the rat race of life, where she became lost— in her work life but, most of all, lost in herself and her own meaning of life.

Realising that her experiences and stories were yelling from within, she put pen to paper and began a transformative journey with her creative poems.

Vicky has always had a love for poetry in many forms and believes this creative way has helped her to understand life in a more profound way.

Vicky has three children and one grandson, whom she loves dearly, and lives in Liverpool with her two dogs (Lexi & Charlie) and her two cats (Otis & Prince). She loves to be out in nature with the birds and will spend many a day walking through her local park and pays many a visit to the beach to hear the vast waters breathe.

Her heart always beats big and strong, not only for people but also for animals. She is always rescuing the strays that turn up at her door, and her utmost dream is to own a home one day with a plot of land and to have many animals. Most of all, she would love to home her biggest passion—DONKEYS. Anyone who knows Vicky knows she has a strong connection to these beautiful animals.

Vicky has a strong belief in people finding the freedom to be themselves and not live their lives through anyone else.

Vicky is now working on other creative projects for the future, which she hopes will take the reader on a journey of empowerment and learning.

Connect with Vicky on Instagram:
@vicky_sneade and @4_theloveofyou

Printed in Dunstable, United Kingdom

71146840R00033